BREAK FREE FROM ANXIOUS ATTACHMENT: CREATING DEEPER RELATIONSHIPS

INTRODUCTION:

For as long as I can remember, relationships have been a source of both joy and deep anxiety. The rollercoaster of emotional highs and lows, the constant fear of abandonment, and the overwhelming need for reassurance—all of these became defining features of my personal and romantic relationships. If you've ever felt trapped by the fear that those you love might leave you, or if you've found yourself constantly seeking validation, then you may recognize yourself in my story. This book is a reflection of that journey: one that has been shaped by my struggle with anxious attachment and years of therapy, healing, and growth.

Insecure attachment, particularly the anxious attachment style, is something that I didn't fully understand until I found myself in relationships that left me feeling more unsettled, more uncertain, and more exhausted than I'd ever imagined. I constantly worried about whether I was enough for the people I loved. I found myself clinging to others for fear of being abandoned, which only created more tension and instability. It wasn't until I began my own therapeutic journey—years of self-reflection, emotional work, and countless hours of therapy—that I began to understand the roots of my anxiety and the behaviors that had held me hostage for so long.

Through this process, I learned that anxious attachment isn't something to be ashamed of, but rather a pattern of behavior and emotional response that can be understood, unlearned, and ultimately transformed. It's been a painful but profoundly liberating journey, and it's one that continues to unfold. In this book, I'll be sharing the tools and strategies that helped me heal and build a more secure sense of self. These are the same tools I've used to break free from the cycle of anxiety and dependence, and I believe they can help you too.

This book isn't meant to replace professional mental health advice, therapy, or medical intervention. I am not a licensed therapist or mental health professional. The advice and strategies I offer are based on my personal experiences, research, and lessons learned throughout my own journey. Every person's path to healing is unique, and if you're struggling with significant emotional distress or trauma, I encourage you to seek the help of a qualified therapist or mental health professional. It is okay to need support, and in fact, it is one of the strongest steps you can take toward healing.

The tools in this book are not a cure-all, nor will they instantly solve everything. Building emotional resilience and healing from anxious attachment takes time, patience, and persistence. However, I believe that the process is worth every step. Just as I have found my way toward greater emotional balance and healthier relationships, I am confident that you can too.

I hope that this book serves as both a guide and a source of comfort as you embark on your own journey of healing. You are not alone in this, and there is a way forward, no matter how difficult the road may seem. Healing is possible, and I am here to walk alongside you through this process.

With gratitude and empathy,

CS Vail

Disclaimer:

The information in this book is based on the author's personal experiences and research. It is not intended to be a substitute for professional mental health care, therapy, or medical advice. If you are struggling with emotional distress or trauma, it is important to seek help from a licensed mental health professional or therapist. The strategies and tools shared in this book are intended to be a supportive resource but should be used in conjunction with professional care if needed.

CHAPTER 1: UNDERSTANDING ANXIOUS ATTACHMENT

"Attachment is the invisible thread that binds us to others—it shapes how we love, connect, and heal."

What is Anxious Attachment?

Anxious attachment is one of the four main attachment styles identified in attachment theory, a psychological framework developed by John Bowlby and Mary Ainsworth. This style develops in childhood when caregivers are inconsistent—sometimes responsive and nurturing, other times distant or unavailable. This inconsistency leads to a persistent fear of abandonment and a strong desire for closeness, often resulting in clingy or overly dependent behaviors in adult relationships.

Key Characteristics of Anxious Attachment:

* Fear of abandonment: A constant worry that your partner may leave.

* Overanalysis: Frequently second-guessing your partner's actions or words.

* Reassurance-seeking: Craving validation and frequent reminders of love or loyalty.

* Difficulty with independence: Feeling uneasy or lost when spending time apart from loved ones.

The Science of Attachment

Attachment is not just emotional—it is deeply rooted in biology. The attachment system is regulated by neurochemical responses in the brain. Oxytocin, often called the "bonding hormone," promotes closeness, while heightened cortisol levels can amplify anxiety when connection feels threatened.

In anxious attachment, this system is hyperactive. Small relationship challenges, like a delayed text or change in tone, can trigger the brain's alarm system, causing emotional distress. Understanding this biological foundation is the first step toward addressing anxious patterns.

How Anxious Attachment Impacts Relationships

People with an anxious attachment style may experience the following in their relationships:

1. Hypervigilance: Constantly scanning for signs of a partner pulling away.

2. Emotional highs and lows: Feeling euphoric when connected, but devastated during perceived disconnection.

3. Conflict avoidance or escalation: Either withdrawing to avoid abandonment or pushing for reassurance in unhealthy ways.

These behaviors, though understandable, can strain relationships, as partners may feel overwhelmed or unable to meet the constant need for reassurance.

Attachment in Action: A Real-Life Scenario

Emily and James:

Emily, a 32-year-old marketing professional, always feels nervous when her boyfriend, James, doesn't reply to her texts immediately. If James mentions needing space, Emily interprets it as a sign he's losing interest. Her anxiety leads her to send multiple follow-up messages, which James finds overwhelming, causing him to withdraw further—a cycle that reinforces Emily's fears.

Emily's pattern illustrates how anxious attachment creates self-fulfilling prophecies: fearing abandonment leads to behaviors that push partners away.

Hope for Healing

The good news is that attachment styles are not fixed. With understanding, effort, and the right tools, anxious individuals can work toward a secure attachment style. Healing starts by recognizing patterns, developing emotional regulation skills, and practicing healthy communication.

Exercises: Understanding Your Style

1. Self-Reflection Questions:

    * How do I react when I feel a loved one is pulling away?

    * What triggers my fears of abandonment in relationships?

    * How do I typically seek reassurance from others?

2. Attachment Style Quiz:

    * Take a quiz to identify your attachment style and better understand its impact on your relationships (e.g., quizzes in Attached or online resources like Psychology Today).

Looking Ahead

This chapter sets the stage for your journey from anxious to secure attachment. In the next chapter, we'll explore how to identify and break free from repetitive patterns that keep you stuck in anxious cycles. Together, we'll build a roadmap to emotional freedom and fulfilling relationships.

CHAPTER 1 FOLLOW UP EXERCISES:

Exercise 1: Map Your Attachment History

This exercise helps readers trace the roots of their anxious attachment style and recognize patterns.

Steps:

1. Reflect on Your Childhood Caregivers:

* Write about how your primary caregivers responded to your emotional needs. Were they consistent, distant, or unpredictable?

* Example prompts:

* "When I was upset as a child, my caregiver would typically ______."

* "I felt most loved when my caregiver ______."

2. Connect the Dots:

* Look for patterns between your childhood experiences and how you currently respond in relationships.

* For instance: "My parent often ignored me when I was upset, so I now feel anxious when my partner is quiet after an argument."

3. Summarize Insights:

* Write 2–3 sentences summarizing how these patterns might influence your current attachment style.

Purpose:

This exercise fosters awareness by connecting early experiences to present behaviors, a crucial step toward change.

Exercise 2: Relationship Audit

This exercise helps you examine your relationship behaviors to identify areas for growth.

Steps:

1. List Your Past Relationships:

   * Create a table with three columns:

      * Relationship: Partner's name or a description (e.g., "college boyfriend").

      * My Behavior: How you typically acted in the relationship.

      * Trigger: Situations or actions that made you feel anxious.

2. Spot Repeating Patterns:

   * Review the table for recurring themes. Ask yourself:

      * "Do I often feel insecure when communication slows down?"

      * "Am I quick to assume my partner will leave during disagreements?"

3. Set a Goal:

   * Write one behavior you'd like to change in future relationships. For example:

      * "I want to pause and self-soothe before asking for reassurance."

Purpose:

This exercise provides a structured way to recognize and address patterns in past relationships, paving the way for healthier behaviors in the future.

CHAPTER 2: RECOGNIZING YOUR PATTERNS

"The first step to breaking free from a cycle is to become aware of it. Patterns only have power over us when we remain unaware of them."

Understanding the Role of Patterns in Attachment

Patterns in relationships are often unconscious, repeated behaviors that we carry over from past experiences. These patterns can stem from childhood interactions with caregivers and significant figures in our lives. In the case of anxious attachment, these patterns often manifest as intense emotional responses to perceived rejection or abandonment, and they tend to show up in romantic relationships, friendships, and even family dynamics.

Recognizing your patterns is crucial because it allows you to consciously decide whether you want to continue these behaviors or change them. It is easy to assume that we are simply "reacting" to what others are doing, but in reality, we are often playing out scripts that were formed long ago.

The Cycle of Anxiety and Reassurance-Seeking

One common pattern in anxious attachment is the cycle of seeking reassurance, often triggered by perceived signs of disinterest or emotional distance from a partner. This can look like:

* Needing constant validation: When your partner doesn't respond immediately to a message, you may feel that they no longer care, prompting you to send follow-up texts, emails, or calls.

* Overanalyzing: You scrutinize every word or gesture for hidden meanings, interpreting neutral behaviors (such as a late reply) as signs of impending abandonment.

* Emotional highs and lows: When reassurance is provided, you feel immense relief and happiness, but when it's not, your anxiety spikes, leading to emotional distress.

These patterns can create a self-fulfilling prophecy. For example, when you become clingy or demanding of reassurance, it may push your partner away, leading to more anxiety and fear, which drives even more of the same behavior.

Case Study: The Cycle of Sarah and Ben

Sarah, a 28-year-old teacher, has been dating Ben for six months. Recently, she noticed that Ben was slower to respond to her texts. She felt a wave of anxiety and wondered if he was losing interest. Sarah immediately texted him several times, asking if everything was okay and if he was upset with her. Ben reassured her, but this didn't alleviate Sarah's fears. Instead, she found herself scrutinizing his replies, trying to decode every message. When Ben didn't immediately return her call one evening, Sarah spent hours feeling anxious, imagining all sorts of negative scenarios. This cycle repeated itself, with Sarah's anxiety and clinginess pushing Ben further away, causing the very emotional distance she feared.

Sarah's story is a common example of the anxious attachment cycle. Her pattern of reassurance-seeking, over analysis, and emotional reactivity, which originated from early experiences with inconsistent caregiving, created a predictable cycle of anxiety in her adult relationships.

The Importance of Self-Awareness

To break free from these patterns, the first step is to become aware of them. This doesn't mean blaming yourself for your feelings or behaviors; rather, it's about recognizing that these patterns can be unlearned with effort and intention. Awareness is the key to shifting from automatic reactions to mindful responses.

Psychologist and attachment theory expert Dr. Diane Poole Heller notes that anxious individuals often repeat behaviors because they don't know another way to seek connection or affection. These behaviors may have been adaptive at one point—helping you cope with emotional neglect or inconsistency—but they no longer serve you in adult relationships 【14】 【16】 .

Once you start recognizing your patterns, you can begin to challenge them and create healthier alternatives. The goal is not to eliminate anxiety or fear, but to develop healthier coping mechanisms that allow you to respond with greater emotional regulation and security.

How to Identify Your Emotional Triggers

Emotional triggers are events or behaviors that activate your attachment system and cause anxiety. These triggers often arise from small, everyday situations, such as:

* A delay in a partner's response.

* A slight change in tone during a conversation.

* A partner needing space or time alone.

* Physical distance or a temporary breakup.

These triggers can activate deep fears of abandonment or rejection, causing disproportionate emotional reactions. Learning to identify these triggers is vital in breaking the cycle of anxiety.

Exercises: Identifying and Challenging Your Patterns

1. The Relationship Timeline:

* Create a timeline of your significant past relationships, both romantic and non-romantic. For each, note the behaviors you typically exhibited (e.g., seeking constant reassurance, withdrawing emotionally, becoming overly clingy, etc.).

* Reflect on whether these behaviors helped or hindered the relationship. Were they reactive or proactive? What impact did they have on the dynamics between you and the other person?

2. Trigger Mapping:

* Make a list of your emotional triggers. For each trigger, write down how you typically respond. For example:

* Trigger: My partner doesn't reply to my text immediately.

* Response: I panic and send multiple texts asking if everything is okay.

* Emotional Reaction: Anxiety, fear of being abandoned.

* Once you've mapped out your triggers, create alternative responses. For instance, you could commit to pausing for five minutes and practicing deep breathing before responding impulsively.

Looking Ahead: Breaking Free from the Cycle

Recognizing your patterns is only the first step toward healing. In the upcoming chapters, we'll discuss how to regulate your emotions, communicate more effectively, and set healthier boundaries. By becoming aware of your patterns and triggers, you're laying the foundation for creating secure, fulfilling relationships.

CHAPTER 2 FOLLOW UP EXERCISES:

Exercise 1: Pattern Recognition Journal

1. Journal Prompt:

* At the end of each day (or after a significant interaction), reflect on the events that triggered your anxiety or attachment-related behaviors.

* What happened?

* How did you feel emotionally (e.g., anxious, fearful, rejected)?

* What thoughts ran through your mind (e.g., "They don't care," or "I'll be abandoned")?

* How did you react (e.g., sent multiple texts, overanalyzed a conversation, sought reassurance)?

2. Pattern Tracking:

* After journaling for a week, look back at your entries. Identify common threads or recurring triggers. Ask yourself:

* Are there specific situations (e.g., when my partner is distant, when communication is delayed) that set off the cycle of anxiety and reassurance-seeking?

* Do certain fears show up repeatedly (e.g., fear of

abandonment, fear of being misunderstood)?

3. Reflection:

* Write a summary of your key observations. What surprised you? Did you notice any behavior that you had not consciously recognized before?

* Write down one new way to respond the next time you face a similar situation.

Purpose:

This exercise helps you become more aware of your attachment behaviors and how they play out daily, which is the first step in making conscious changes. By tracking your patterns, you gain insight into your emotional triggers, making it easier to break the cycle.

Exercise 2: Thought Reframing Challenge

Anxious attachment is often rooted in distorted thoughts about relationships. This exercise helps you challenge and reframe negative thoughts, creating healthier, more realistic beliefs.

Steps:

1. Identify Negative Thought Patterns:

* Think back to the last time you experienced significant anxiety in a relationship (e.g., a missed call, an argument). Write down the negative thoughts you had at that moment, such as:

* "They're going to leave me."

* "They must be mad at me."

* "If they don't call back, they don't care."

2. Challenge the Thought:

* For each negative thought, ask yourself:

* "Is this thought based on facts or assumptions?"

* "What evidence do I have to support this thought?"

* "Have I been in similar situations before where things worked out?"

* "What is a more balanced or positive way of thinking about this situation?"

* Example Reframing:

* Negative Thought: "They're going to leave me if I don't hear from them soon."

* Reframed Thought: "I don't know what they're thinking right now. There could be many reasons they haven't responded. I can trust that we'll communicate when the time is right."

3. Practice Reframing:

* Over the course of a week, keep a record of your anxious thoughts and practice reframing them. Each time you catch yourself feeling anxious or thinking negatively, pause and replace that thought with a healthier, more balanced one.

4. Reflect:

* At the end of the week, write a brief reflection:

* How did it feel to challenge your thoughts?

* Were you able to reduce anxiety in certain situations by reframing your thoughts?

* What new patterns do you want to continue practicing?

Purpose:

This exercise helps you retrain your brain to recognize and correct distorted thinking. It builds emotional resilience by shifting from anxious, fearful thinking toward a more grounded and balanced perspective, reducing anxiety and enabling healthier responses to relationship triggers.

CHAPTER 3: MINDFULNESS AS A FOUNDATION

"The present moment is the only time over which we have control. Learning to be present allows us to break free from the worries of the past and the anxieties of the future."

What is Mindfulness?

Mindfulness is the practice of paying deliberate attention to the present moment, without judgment. It involves observing your thoughts, feelings, and sensations as they arise, without getting caught up in them. For people with anxious attachment, mindfulness can be particularly powerful because it offers a way to ground yourself in the present, reducing the emotional spirals caused by past experiences or worries about the future.

Mindfulness is not about eliminating emotions or forcing yourself to "think positive." Rather, it is about creating space between your experiences and reactions, allowing you to respond with greater calm and clarity. Studies have shown that mindfulness reduces anxiety, increases emotional regulation, and fosters a sense of well-being (Kabat-Zinn, 1990; Siegel, 2007).

The Benefits of Mindfulness for Anxious Attachment

For those with anxious attachment, mindfulness offers several key benefits:

1. Emotional Regulation: It helps you detach from intense emotional reactions, allowing you to process emotions more calmly and rationally.

2. Breaking the Cycle of Overthinking: Mindfulness helps you stay present, rather than getting lost in worry or rumination about what might happen in your relationships.

3. Creating Space for Self-Soothing: Instead of immediately seeking reassurance from others, mindfulness allows you to comfort yourself first, reducing dependence on external validation.

Mindfulness helps disrupt the cycle of anxiety by training your brain to recognize when you're spiraling. Rather than allowing yourself to get lost in the emotions of fear and doubt, you can step back and observe your thoughts from a place of neutrality.

Mindfulness and Attachment Styles

Research shows that mindfulness can positively influence attachment patterns. For those with anxious attachment, it allows individuals to notice when they are becoming anxious and gives them the tools to manage their emotional responses. Mindfulness doesn't require changing how you feel—it teaches you how to manage those feelings effectively (Shaver & Mikulincer, 2002; Heller, 2018).

For example, instead of immediately assuming that a partner's delayed response is a sign of abandonment, mindfulness enables you to recognize that this thought is based on anxiety, not fact. With practice, you can choose not to react impulsively and allow space for more balanced thoughts.

Getting Started with Mindfulness

If you're new to mindfulness, it can seem overwhelming at first. The good news is that mindfulness is a skill that can be developed over time with regular practice. The more you practice mindfulness, the more you will notice its positive effects on your emotional well-being.

How to Practice Mindfulness Daily

To build mindfulness into your daily routine, try these tips:

* Start Small: Aim for just 5-10 minutes of mindfulness practice each day. You can gradually increase the duration as it becomes easier.

* Incorporate Mindfulness into Daily Activities: Whether you're eating, walking, or washing dishes, try to be fully present in whatever you're doing. Pay attention to the sensory experience (taste, touch, sound).

* Use Reminders: Set reminders on your phone or sticky notes around your home to pause and check in with yourself throughout the day.

Mindfulness doesn't require a lot of time, but it does require consistency. Even a few minutes each day can have a powerful impact on reducing anxiety and improving emotional regulation.

The Journey Ahead

Mindfulness is a foundation for emotional healing. By learning to ground yourself in the present moment, you will be able to manage your anxious feelings with greater ease and begin to build the skills needed for secure attachment. In the next chapters, we will build on this mindfulness foundation, learning how to regulate emotions, communicate more effectively, and set healthy boundaries in relationships.

The 5-4-3-2-1 Grounding Exercise

The 5-4-3-2-1 grounding technique is a simple mindfulness tool to help you stay present and distract your mind from anxious thoughts.

Steps:

1. 5 Things You Can See: Look around you and identify five things you can see. Name them aloud or in your mind.

2. 4 Things You Can Feel: Pay attention to your body and note four physical sensations. It could be the texture of your clothing, the temperature of the air, or the feeling of your feet on the ground.

3. 3 Things You Can Hear: Focus on three sounds in your environment. These might be the hum of a fan, birds outside, or the sound of your breath.

4. 2 Things You Can Smell: Take note of two scents you can detect. If you're in an environment without a strong smell, take a deep breath and notice the subtle smells around you.

5. 1 Thing You Can Taste: Focus on the taste in your mouth, whether it's the lingering taste of food or the freshness of your breath.

Purpose:
This exercise is especially helpful in moments of anxiety or overwhelming emotions. It allows you to reconnect with your environment, bringing you back into the present moment and distracting your mind from anxious thoughts (Heller, 2018; Kabat-Zinn, 1990).

How to Practice Mindfulness Daily

To build mindfulness into your daily routine, try these tips:

* Start Small: Aim for just 5-10 minutes of mindfulness practice

each day. You can gradually increase the duration as it becomes easier.

* Incorporate Mindfulness into Daily Activities: Whether you're eating, walking, or washing dishes, try to be fully present in whatever you’re doing. Pay attention to the sensory experience (taste, touch, sound).

* Use Reminders: Set reminders on your phone or sticky notes around your home to pause and check in with yourself throughout the day.

The Journey Ahead

Mindfulness is a foundation for emotional healing. By learning to ground yourself in the present moment, you will be able to manage your anxious feelings with greater ease and begin to build the skills needed for secure attachment. In the next chapters, we will build on this mindfulness foundation, learning how to regulate emotions, communicate more effectively, and set healthy boundaries in relationships.

CHAPTER 3 FOLLOW-UP EXERCISES:

Exercise 1: Mindful Breathing Practice

One of the simplest and most effective ways to return to the present moment is through mindful breathing. This exercise can be done anywhere and anytime you begin to feel anxious or overwhelmed by emotions.

Steps:

1. Find a Comfortable Position: Sit in a quiet space, or if you are in motion (e.g., walking), slow your pace to allow for focus.

2. Focus on Your Breath: Close your eyes and take a slow, deep breath in through your nose. Allow your lungs to fully fill, hold briefly, and then exhale slowly through your mouth.

3. Counting Breaths: As you inhale, silently count "1," and as you exhale, count "2." Continue counting up to 10, then begin again at 1. If your mind wanders, gently bring it back to your breath without judgment.

4. Full Awareness: With each breath, focus your attention on the sensation of air entering and leaving your body. Notice how the breath feels—cool as it enters, warm as it exits.

5. Continue for 5-10 Minutes: Practice for a few minutes or until you feel more grounded and calm. You can gradually extend the time as it becomes more comfortable.

Purpose:

Mindful breathing helps anchor you to the present and calms the nervous system, which is often in overdrive for those with anxious attachment. It provides a quick reset when anxiety arises, allowing you to respond to situations with more clarity and emotional stability (Kabat-Zinn, 1990; Heller, 2018).

Exercise 2: Creating A Mindfulness Ritual

Incorporating mindfulness into a daily ritual can help you maintain a grounded, present state throughout the day. This exercise encourages you to design a personalized ritual that brings you back to yourself, promoting calm and reducing anxiety.

Steps:

1. Choose a Daily Activity: Select an activity that you do regularly, such as having a cup of tea, journaling, taking a walk, or brushing your teeth. This will become your mindfulness ritual.

2. Set an Intention: Before you begin the activity, take a moment to set an intention. This could be something like, "I will focus on the sensory experience of this moment," or "I will notice any thoughts that arise and let them pass without judgment."

3. Engage Fully: As you go through the motions of the activity, engage all of your senses. If you're drinking tea, notice its warmth, smell, and taste. If you're walking, focus on the feeling of your feet on the ground and the movement of your body.

4. Reflect on the Experience: After completing the activity, reflect briefly on how it felt to be fully present. Did you feel more relaxed? Were you able to let go of anxious thoughts for a while?

Purpose:

By making mindfulness a regular part of your day, you're training yourself to stay present, which can be particularly beneficial when dealing with attachment anxiety. This ritual serves as a reminder to stay in the moment and reduces the tendency to ruminate on past or future concerns (Kabat-Zinn, 1990; Heller, 2018).

CHAPTER 4: DEVELOPING HEALTHY COMMUNICATION SKILLS

"The quality of your communication directly influences the quality of your relationships."

The Role of Communication in Relationships

Effective communication is the cornerstone of healthy relationships, particularly for individuals with anxious attachment. As someone with anxious attachment may experience heightened sensitivity to perceived rejection or emotional distance, developing strong communication skills is essential for expressing needs, managing conflict, and building trust.

Research highlights that anxious individuals often have difficulty articulating their feelings or fears, leading to misunderstandings and emotional distress (Mikulincer & Shaver, 2016). They might struggle with over-explaining or seeking constant reassurance, which can strain relationships. Therefore, learning how to communicate clearly, assertively, and calmly is crucial for creating a balanced dynamic in relationships (Shaver & Mikulincer, 2002).

The Foundations of Effective Communication

There are several key principles that form the foundation of effective communication. For individuals with anxious attachment, these principles can help manage emotional reactivity and improve the quality of interactions:

1. Active Listening: This involves paying full attention to what the other person is saying without interrupting or judging. Active listening encourages empathy, understanding, and validation (Brownell, 2012).

2. I-Statements: Rather than blaming or accusing, use "I" statements to express how you feel. For example, "I feel anxious when I don't hear from you" is more effective than "You never text me back" (Gottman, 1999).

3. Nonverbal Communication: Body language, facial expressions, and tone of voice can often convey more than words. Being aware of these nonverbal cues is crucial in expressing yourself clearly and understanding your partner's emotions (Mehrabian, 1972).

4. Clarity and Conciseness: Being clear and to the point can prevent misunderstandings and reduce unnecessary emotional tension. When you feel anxious, it can be easy to ramble or say things you don't mean. Practicing clarity can help you stay focused on your message (Gottman, 1999).

5. Timing and Environment: Choosing the right time and setting for important conversations can help both parties remain calm and receptive. Avoid discussing sensitive topics during stressful or emotionally charged moments (Duck, 1994).

Common Communication Barriers for Anxious Attachment

While the principles of healthy communication are universal, individuals with anxious attachment may face unique challenges in this area. These challenges stem from deep-seated fears of abandonment and emotional insecurity, which can manifest in several ways:

1. Fear of Rejection: Those with anxious attachment may avoid expressing their true feelings out of fear that their partner will not respond positively. This can lead to emotional withdrawal or passive-aggressive behaviors (Hazan & Shaver, 1987).

2. Over-Reliance on Reassurance: Anxious individuals often seek constant reassurance from their partners, believing that this will alleviate their fears. However, this pattern can be draining and counterproductive, as it may place undue pressure on the other person to provide validation (Mikulincer & Shaver, 2007).

3. Difficulty with Boundaries: Establishing and respecting boundaries can be challenging for someone with anxious attachment. Without healthy boundaries, individuals may become overly dependent on their partner, leading to imbalances in the relationship (Siegel, 2007).

4. Emotional Overload: In moments of anxiety, individuals may struggle to articulate their emotions effectively. This can result in emotional outbursts or withdrawing from the conversation entirely, which further complicates communication (Shaver & Mikulincer, 2002).

Developing Communication Skills for Anxious Attachment

To navigate these barriers, individuals with anxious attachment can develop a variety of communication strategies:

1. Practice Self-Awareness: Begin by noticing your emotional reactions and triggers. When you feel anxious or overwhelmed, take a moment to pause and reflect on your feelings. This pause

allows you to regain control of your emotional response before speaking (Thompson, 2014).

2. Use Grounding Techniques: Before engaging in a difficult conversation, try using mindfulness techniques to ground yourself. This might involve deep breathing, a body scan, or focusing on the present moment. Grounding techniques can help reduce anxiety and enable clearer, more thoughtful communication (Kabat-Zinn, 1990).

3. Learn to Self-Soothe: When you feel the urge to seek immediate reassurance or escalate the situation, practice self-soothing strategies. This could include affirmations, relaxation exercises, or even taking a short walk to cool off (Heller, 2018). By calming yourself first, you create space for healthier communication with your partner.

4. Set Healthy Boundaries: It's important to communicate your emotional needs and establish boundaries with others. This helps you feel secure in the relationship without becoming overly dependent on your partner for validation. Assertive communication can be learned and practiced through small, everyday interactions (Linehan, 1993).

5. Seek Feedback: After important conversations, ask for feedback from your partner. Did they feel heard? Was the message clear? Openly discussing communication dynamics can help identify patterns and areas for improvement (Gottman, 1999).

Communication Exercises for Anxious Attachment

The "I Feel" Statements Practice

This exercise helps you practice using "I" statements to communicate your emotions without triggering defensiveness in your partner. Practice the following steps:

1. Take a moment to identify how you're feeling.

2. Use the formula: "I feel [emotion] when [situation]. I need [specific request]."

Example: "I feel anxious when you don't respond to my texts. I need reassurance that you're okay."

3. Repeat this process with different situations where you've felt emotionally reactive. Try to identify patterns in how you communicate.

Purpose:
This exercise encourages emotional honesty and clarity. By taking responsibility for your feelings without blaming others, you can foster more open, constructive conversations.

Role-Playing Difficult Conversations

Role-playing is a powerful way to practice communication in a low-stakes environment. Find a trusted friend or therapist to help you practice a conversation you anticipate might trigger anxiety.

1. Decide on a difficult conversation you've been avoiding, such as setting a boundary or expressing a need.

2. Take turns playing both yourself and the other person. Practice expressing your feelings and needs clearly and assertively.

3. Pay attention to your tone of voice, body language, and emotional responses. Try to stay calm and focused, even if the conversation becomes uncomfortable.

Purpose:
Role-playing can help reduce anxiety about difficult conversations by familiarizing you with the process of healthy communication. It builds confidence and prepares you for real-world interactions.

Conclusion: Strengthening Communication for Lasting Change

Mastering communication skills is not a quick fix, but a long-term investment in your relationships. For individuals with anxious attachment, the ability to communicate openly, assertively, and calmly can transform how you relate to others and how others relate to you. With practice, these skills can reduce anxiety, build trust, and create more secure, fulfilling connections.

CHAPTER 4 FOLLOW UP EXERCISES:

Exercise 1: Reflection And Feedback Journaling

Reflecting on your communication and emotional responses in a journal can provide invaluable insights into your patterns of behavior. This exercise involves writing down and analyzing your interactions to help identify both strengths and areas for growth in your communication skills.

Steps:

1. Choose a Recent Interaction: Select a recent conversation in which you felt emotionally triggered, anxious, or misunderstood.

2. Describe the Event: Write down the details of the conversation, including your emotional state, what you said, and how the other person responded.
Example: "I asked my partner to reassure me about our relationship, and they seemed frustrated. I felt rejected, but I didn't express that well."

3. Analyze the Communication: Reflect on what went well and what could be improved. Consider the following:

 * Did you express your feelings clearly?

 * Did you use "I feel" statements?

 * Did your body language and tone align with your words?

 * Did you ask for what you needed directly?

4. Identify Emotional Triggers: Identify any specific emotional triggers that came up during the conversation. Were there moments where anxiety increased? How did it affect your communication?

5. Feedback to Yourself: Write down one thing you can improve in future conversations.
Example: "Next time, I will focus on using 'I feel' statements instead of seeking reassurance. I will also take a moment to breathe before reacting if I feel anxious."

Purpose:

This exercise encourages self-awareness and emotional growth. By reviewing past conversations and providing yourself with constructive feedback, you can build confidence in your communication skills and make gradual improvements. Over time, this practice helps you better manage emotional triggers and communicate with greater clarity (Thompson, 2014; Mikulincer & Shaver, 2007).

Exercise 2: The Calm Down Script

For individuals with anxious attachment, moments of emotional overload or anxiety can make it difficult to communicate effectively. The Calm Down Script is designed to help you pause, regulate your emotions, and communicate in a clear, measured way when emotions feel overwhelming.

Steps:

1. Acknowledge the Emotion: When you feel anxious or upset, take a deep breath and acknowledge the emotion you are experiencing.
Example: "I am feeling anxious right now."

2. Pause Before Reacting: If you feel the urge to immediately react (such as demanding reassurance, withdrawing, or arguing), pause for a moment. You can say to yourself, "I need a moment to gather my thoughts."

3. Use the Script: Follow the script below to communicate your feelings in a calm and non-confrontational way.
Example:
"I'm feeling anxious about [situation]. I need a little time to process this. I'll be back in [set time, such as 5 minutes]. Please bear with me."

4. Return to the Conversation: After the agreed-upon time, return to the conversation with a clearer mind. Use "I feel" statements to express your emotions and needs.

Purpose:

This script helps individuals with anxious attachment avoid impulsive reactions that might escalate tension. By taking a break and clearly expressing the need for space or understanding, the conversation can continue in a more constructive and balanced manner (Brownell, 2012; Gottman, 1999). It fosters emotional regulation and supports healthier interactions in relationships.

CHAPTER 5: CULTIVATING SECURE ATTACHMENT: MOVING FROM ANXIETY TO SECURITY

"The strongest relationships are built on trust, understanding, and secure attachment."

The Journey from Anxious to Secure Attachment

For individuals with anxious attachment, the goal of cultivating secure attachment involves developing emotional self-sufficiency and fostering relationships that promote mutual understanding, trust, and consistency. Secure attachment is characterized by a healthy balance of intimacy and independence, with partners able to express vulnerability without fear of abandonment (Hazan & Shaver, 1987; Mikulincer & Shaver, 2016).

Moving from anxious to secure attachment is a gradual process that requires self-awareness, emotional regulation, and the development of healthy relationship patterns. This chapter will explore key strategies for fostering secure attachment and offer practical tools for individuals with anxious attachment to build stronger, more stable connections with themselves and others.

Understanding Secure Attachment

Secure attachment is the most adaptive style of attachment, where individuals feel safe, supported, and valued in relationships. People with secure attachment are comfortable with both intimacy and independence, and they maintain healthy emotional boundaries (Bowlby, 1969). They have learned to trust others and themselves, and they can cope with the ups and downs of relationships without becoming overwhelmed by anxiety or fear of abandonment (Shaver & Mikulincer, 2002).

In contrast to anxious attachment, secure individuals do not feel the need for constant reassurance or validation. They are comfortable with both giving and receiving love and support, and they tend to manage conflict in a healthy, constructive manner. Achieving secure attachment involves developing a deeper understanding of how attachment styles manifest in relationships and taking deliberate steps to nurture healthier patterns.

Building Trust and Consistency

One of the most critical components of secure attachment is the presence of trust. For individuals with anxious attachment, trust can be difficult to establish, as they often fear rejection or abandonment. Rebuilding trust in relationships begins with fostering consistency in emotional responses, actions, and communication (Mikulincer & Shaver, 2016).

Research by Gottman (1999) suggests that the foundation of trust in a relationship is built on consistent emotional support and reliability. This means that, over time, partners must show that they can be relied upon for comfort and reassurance during moments of vulnerability or distress. Trust is not something that is built overnight; rather, it is cultivated through ongoing emotional attunement and a willingness to respond to each other's needs.

Self-Awareness: Understanding Your Attachment Patterns

An important step toward building secure attachment is increasing self-awareness of one's own attachment style. For individuals with anxious attachment, this means recognizing when anxiety arises and understanding the triggers that fuel attachment-related fears. The more aware you are of your emotional patterns, the better you can manage your responses in relationships (Shaver & Mikulincer, 2007).

This process involves examining the roots of anxious attachment —often stemming from early childhood experiences or past relational dynamics—and understanding how these early experiences influence adult behaviors (Bowlby, 1973). With this awareness, individuals can begin to interrupt maladaptive patterns, such as seeking excessive reassurance, overanalyzing interactions, or becoming overwhelmed by fears of abandonment.

Developing Emotional Regulation Skills

Emotional regulation is the ability to manage and modulate emotional responses in a way that fosters healthy relationships. For individuals with anxious attachment, emotional regulation is often a critical area for growth. The intensity of emotional responses can make it difficult to engage in calm, rational communication, especially when feeling threatened or insecure (Gross, 2002; Thompson, 2014).

One effective way to regulate emotions is through mindfulness practices, which have been shown to improve emotional awareness and decrease anxiety (Kabat-Zinn, 1990). Mindfulness allows individuals to observe their emotional responses without judgment or reaction, creating space between a trigger and the emotional response. This space provides an opportunity to choose a more measured, thoughtful response, rather than being controlled by overwhelming feelings of fear or insecurity.

Building Healthy Boundaries

Establishing and respecting healthy boundaries is essential for cultivating secure attachment. Individuals with anxious attachment may struggle with boundary-setting, as they often feel the urge to merge with their partner or become overly dependent on them for emotional support (Siegel, 2007). However, secure attachment thrives in relationships where both individuals can maintain a sense of individuality while still offering emotional support and connection.

Setting boundaries is about recognizing your own needs and desires while respecting the needs of others. This means being able to say "no" when necessary, expressing your own emotions without guilt, and ensuring that both partners have space to grow and develop independently. Healthy boundaries provide a sense of safety and autonomy in a relationship, which is crucial for the development of secure attachment (Linehan, 1993).

Fostering Healthy Interdependence

While secure attachment involves a healthy balance of independence and dependence, fostering interdependence—where partners rely on each other in mutually supportive ways—is key to developing secure attachment. Individuals with anxious attachment may initially find it challenging to balance their need for closeness with the desire for autonomy. However, with practice, it is possible to create a dynamic where both partners can meet each other's emotional needs while maintaining their individuality (Hazan & Shaver, 1987).

Interdependence is not about dependency or codependency,

but about creating a relational dynamic where both partners contribute to each other's well-being in meaningful ways. This is achieved through clear communication, emotional support, and an understanding that both individuals can provide and receive care, without feeling overwhelmed or overly reliant on one another.

Strategies for Cultivating Secure Attachment

To support the development of secure attachment, consider the following strategies:

1. Practice Mindfulness and Emotional Regulation: Use mindfulness techniques to build awareness of your emotional responses. This can help you manage anxiety and stay grounded during emotionally charged moments (Kabat-Zinn, 1990).

2. Work on Building Trust: Engage in actions that demonstrate reliability and consistency, such as following through on commitments, being emotionally available, and showing empathy during challenging times (Gottman, 1999).

3. Communicate Openly and Honestly: Use direct communication to express your feelings and needs. Share your emotional experiences and be open to your partner's perspective (Brownell, 2012).

4. Seek Professional Support: Therapy, especially emotionally focused therapy (EFT), can help individuals with anxious attachment explore the roots of their attachment style and work toward building more secure relational patterns (Johnson, 2004).

5. Build Healthy Boundaries: Practice identifying and respecting your own boundaries, as well as your partner's. Boundaries are essential for maintaining a healthy sense of self in relationships (Siegel, 2007).

6. Engage in Self-Reflection: Reflect on your attachment history and how it influences your current relationships. Understanding the root causes of your anxious attachment can help you develop

healthier patterns of behavior (Bowlby, 1969).

Conclusion: The Path to Secure Attachment

Cultivating secure attachment is a gradual process that involves developing emotional self-sufficiency, building trust, and learning to communicate openly and honestly. It requires practice, patience, and a commitment to emotional growth. With time, individuals with anxious attachment can develop the skills and strategies needed to foster secure, balanced relationships.

CHAPTER 5 FOLLOW UP EXPERCISES

Exercise 1: The Attachment Reflection Journal

One of the most important steps in cultivating secure attachment is understanding your personal attachment patterns and how they affect your relationships. The Attachment Reflection Journal helps you examine your interactions and emotional responses through the lens of your attachment style, allowing you to pinpoint areas for growth and practice the behaviors that lead to secure attachment.

Steps:

1. Identify an Emotional Trigger: Reflect on a recent situation where you felt anxious, rejected, or insecure in your relationship. Write down the situation and your initial emotional response.
Example: "I felt overwhelmed when my partner didn't respond to my text right away. I started to feel anxious, thinking they were pulling away."

2. Examine the Attachment Pattern: Ask yourself:

* What did I fear in this situation?

* How did my attachment style influence my reaction?

* Did I express my needs in a healthy way, or did I fall back into old patterns like seeking reassurance or withdrawing?
Write down your reflections on how your attachment style manifested in the situation.

3. Analyze and Challenge the Reaction: Identify any negative or unhelpful thoughts you had. For example, "If they don't respond, they must not care about me." Challenge these thoughts by writing more balanced or realistic alternatives.
Example: "They might be busy or distracted. It doesn't mean they don't care about me."

4. Create an Action Plan for the Future: Write down one or two steps you can take next time you experience a similar trigger to respond more securely.
Example: "Next time, I will take a deep breath and wait before sending a follow-up message. I'll remind myself that my partner is reliable, and we have a solid connection."

Purpose:

This exercise encourages self-awareness and mindfulness, which are key in transforming anxious attachment patterns. It helps individuals identify and challenge irrational fears, practice more secure ways of thinking, and engage in healthier relational behaviors (Mikulincer & Shaver, 2007; Siegel, 2007).

Exercise 2: The Secure Attachment Role-Play

Role-playing can be an effective way to practice new communication skills and experiment with responding more securely in relational scenarios. This exercise allows you to simulate emotionally charged situations and practice responding in a calm, balanced manner, which can build confidence and reinforce secure attachment behaviors.

Steps:

1. Select a Common Triggering Scenario: Think of a situation in which you often feel anxious or insecure in relationships. This might be when your partner is distant, when there's a conflict, or when you feel ignored or unimportant.

2. Partner Up: If possible, work with a trusted friend, family member, or therapist who can play the role of your partner. If you're doing this alone, you can still role-play by imagining the conversation and speaking aloud.

3. Role-Play the Situation: Begin the role-play, with you acting as the person with anxious attachment and your partner acting as your significant other. Start with the scenario where you feel triggered.
Example: "I feel anxious because I haven't heard from you all day. Are you mad at me?"

4. Practice Secure Responses: Now, practice responding with more secure attachment behaviors. For example, instead of immediately seeking reassurance, you might say, "I'm feeling anxious right now, but I trust that you care about me. Can we talk about it when you're free?"
Focus on expressing your feelings clearly and directly, while also maintaining emotional regulation and healthy boundaries.

5. Debrief: After the role-play, discuss the experience with your partner (or reflect on it if you were role-playing alone). What did you do well? What would you like to improve next time? Write

down your insights in a journal for future reference.

Purpose:

This exercise builds confidence in using secure attachment strategies in real-life situations. By practicing these skills in a safe, controlled environment, individuals with anxious attachment can learn to respond more effectively to their triggers and foster healthier relational dynamics (Brownell, 2012; Johnson, 2004).

Both follow up exercises are designed to deepen the practice of cultivating secure attachment by increasing self-awareness, improving emotional regulation, and enhancing communication skills. Through reflection and role-playing, individuals can reinforce the healthy behaviors necessary for building more secure, stable relationships.

CHAPTER 6: BUILDING A SECURE RELATIONSHIP WITH YOURSELF: NURTURING SELF-LOVE AND SELF-WORTH

"Before you can build a secure relationship with others, you must first cultivate a secure relationship with yourself."

The Role of Self-Worth in Attachment

One of the most powerful ways to shift from anxious attachment toward secure attachment is to cultivate a strong sense of self-worth. For individuals with anxious attachment, self-worth is often tied to the approval and validation of others. This reliance on external validation can perpetuate feelings of insecurity and anxiety in relationships. To develop secure attachment, it is essential to begin by fostering self-love and recognizing that you are inherently worthy of love, respect, and care—whether or not others affirm this (Neff, 2011; Gilbert, 2009).

Self-worth is the internal belief in your value, independent of your relationships or accomplishments. It is the understanding that you are valuable simply because you exist. This concept is foundational in the development of secure attachment because it shifts the focus away from seeking constant external reassurance and toward developing internal validation and emotional independence (Harter, 2012).

The Relationship Between Self-Worth and Attachment Style

Research has shown that individuals with anxious attachment often struggle with low self-esteem and have a heightened sensitivity to perceived rejection or criticism. They may seek validation from others in an effort to manage feelings of inadequacy or unworthiness (Mikulincer & Shaver, 2007). However, when self-worth is grounded in internal validation, rather than in the behaviors of others, individuals are better able to withstand challenges in their relationships without spiraling into anxiety or self-doubt (Shaver & Mikulincer, 2016).

Building a healthy sense of self-worth is crucial because it allows individuals to experience love and connection in relationships without depending on the constant approval or reassurance of others. This transformation is an essential step toward secure attachment.

Developing Self-Love: Practical Steps

Self-love is not about narcissism or selfishness; rather, it involves treating yourself with the same care, respect, and compassion that you would offer to a loved one. When we practice self-love, we are better able to set boundaries, manage our emotions, and build healthy relationships with others. For individuals with anxious attachment, self-love can serve as the antidote to feelings of inadequacy and the fear of abandonment.

Here are some key steps to foster self-love:

1. Practice Self-Compassion: Self-compassion involves treating yourself kindly in moments of struggle, rather than being self-critical. When you face setbacks or make mistakes, approach yourself with understanding and warmth, just as you would treat a friend (Neff, 2011). Self-compassion helps mitigate the negative emotional states that often accompany anxious attachment, such as shame or guilt.

2. Challenge Negative Self-Talk: Individuals with anxious attachment often engage in negative self-talk that reinforces feelings of unworthiness or fear of rejection. Begin to notice when negative thoughts arise and replace them with positive, affirming statements about yourself. For example, replace "I'm not good enough" with "I am deserving of love and respect." Cognitive restructuring techniques can be helpful in transforming these patterns (Beck, 2011).

3. Celebrate Your Strengths: Take time to acknowledge your personal strengths and accomplishments. Creating a list of your positive qualities and achievements can help counterbalance the negative self-perceptions often associated with anxious attachment. Focus on the things you do well, rather than only highlighting areas for improvement.

4. Engage in Self-Care: Practicing self-care means actively nurturing your physical, emotional, and mental health. This could involve setting aside time for hobbies, engaging in physical activities, practicing mindfulness, or simply resting. Prioritizing self-care helps reinforce the belief that you are worthy of time, attention, and love.

5. Set Healthy Boundaries: Building self-worth also involves understanding and asserting your needs. Setting clear, healthy

boundaries is a form of self-respect that promotes emotional independence and strengthens your sense of self. Healthy boundaries allow you to maintain a balanced relationship with yourself and others, ensuring that your emotional well-being is protected (Linehan, 1993; Siegel, 2007).

The Power of Internal Validation

For individuals with anxious attachment, the desire for external validation can often feel overwhelming. The need for constant reassurance or approval from others is tied to feelings of insecurity and the fear of abandonment. However, when you start to cultivate internal validation, you free yourself from the need for constant affirmation from others. Internal validation involves acknowledging your own worth, validating your own feelings, and affirming your value from within, regardless of external circumstances (Brené Brown, 2012).

One powerful technique for building internal validation is to practice self-reflection. Take time each day to reflect on your thoughts, emotions, and actions without judgment. Allow yourself to simply be, without constantly seeking approval or reassurance from others. This can help you recognize that your worth does not depend on others' opinions or actions.

Overcoming the Fear of Abandonment

A common challenge for individuals with anxious attachment is the fear of abandonment. This fear often stems from early childhood experiences of inconsistent caregiving or neglect, leading to a heightened sensitivity to any perceived emotional distance from others. Overcoming this fear involves building emotional resilience and learning to trust yourself and others (Hazan & Shaver, 1987; Bowlby, 1969).

In order to overcome the fear of abandonment, it is important to:

1. Reframe Negative Beliefs: The fear of abandonment is often

rooted in negative, irrational beliefs about relationships. For example, individuals with anxious attachment may believe that if their partner doesn't immediately respond to a message, it's a sign that they are pulling away or that they will eventually leave. By reframing these thoughts, individuals can challenge these beliefs and replace them with more balanced perspectives (Beck, 2011).

2. Practice Emotional Regulation: When the fear of abandonment arises, it is crucial to practice emotional regulation techniques such as deep breathing, grounding exercises, or mindfulness. These tools can help you stay calm in the face of anxiety and prevent your emotions from overwhelming you (Gross, 2002).

3. Build Trust Gradually: Trust is a crucial component in overcoming the fear of abandonment. To build trust, focus on developing open, honest communication with your partner and demonstrate reliability in your own actions. Over time, as you see that your partner can be counted on, the fear of abandonment will lessen.

Conclusion: Reclaiming Your Worth

Reclaiming your sense of self-worth and building self-love is a powerful way to move from anxious attachment to secure attachment. By practicing self-compassion, setting healthy boundaries, and learning to validate yourself internally, you begin to develop emotional resilience and independence. The more you reinforce the belief that you are deserving of love and respect, the less dependent you will become on the approval of others. This shift fosters the security and stability needed for healthy, fulfilling relationships.

CHAPTER 6 FOLLOW-UP EXERCISES:

Exercise 1: The Daily Affirmation Ritual

One powerful way to build and reinforce self-worth is through the practice of positive affirmations. This exercise involves creating a personalized affirmation ritual that allows you to remind yourself daily of your inherent value and deserving of love, respect, and happiness. This can help transform negative self-talk patterns and shift your mindset toward greater self-acceptance and confidence.

Steps:

1. Create Your Affirmations: Write down five positive affirmations that resonate with you. These should focus on your inherent worth and capacity for love and growth. Examples include:

   * "I am worthy of love and respect."

   * "I trust in my ability to overcome challenges."

   * "I am enough just as I am."

   * "I choose to love myself unconditionally."

   * "My worth is not dependent on others' opinions."

Feel free to personalize these statements to align with your specific needs and experiences.

2. Create a Daily Ritual: Set aside a few minutes each day—preferably in the morning or before bed—when you can focus

on yourself. This could be during a quiet moment, while looking in the mirror, or even as you journal. Repeat each affirmation slowly and with intention. As you say them, visualize what each affirmation means for you and how it makes you feel. Imagine yourself fully embodying these beliefs.

3. Write Your Reflection: After repeating your affirmations, write down any feelings or thoughts that arise. Did any affirmation feel particularly powerful? Did any cause resistance or discomfort? Use this reflection to identify areas where you may need to do further work on self-love or where you are already thriving.

4. Repeat Daily: Commit to practicing this affirmation ritual daily. Over time, these affirmations will help to internalize a sense of self-worth and reduce the need for external validation.

Purpose:

Affirmations help rewire negative thought patterns by affirming your value and importance. This practice fosters internal validation and strengthens self-love, which is vital for secure attachment (Neff, 2011; Gilbert, 2009).

Exercise 2: The Self-Worth Vision Board

Creating a vision board is a creative and visually impactful way to reinforce your sense of self-worth and affirm your value. The process of making a vision board allows you to focus on the positive aspects of yourself and your life, visually representing what you want to affirm about who you are and the relationships you want to nurture.

Steps:

1. Gather Materials: You will need a large piece of poster board or cardboard, magazines or printouts, scissors, glue, or tape. You can also include personal photos, quotes, or drawings.

2. Reflect on Your Self-Worth: Take some time to reflect on what you value most about yourself and what qualities make you feel worthy of love, care, and respect. Write down these attributes —whether they are emotional, physical, intellectual, or spiritual. Examples might include "kind," "resilient," "creative," or "worthy of peace and happiness."

3. Select Images and Words: Flip through magazines or use online resources to find images, words, and quotes that represent these qualities or that inspire self-love. You might find pictures that reflect confidence, strength, peace, or growth. Collect any visual representations of your self-worth.

4. Create Your Vision Board: Arrange the images and words on your board, focusing on how they reflect your value and strengths. Once you are happy with the layout, glue or tape the images into place.

5. Use the Vision Board Daily: Place the vision board somewhere you can see it every day—perhaps in your bedroom, office, or a personal space. Take a moment each day to reflect on the images and words, reminding yourself of your intrinsic worth and the value you bring to the world.

6. Update Regularly: As your self-worth evolves, you can add new elements to the vision board, adjusting it as your beliefs about yourself grow stronger.

Purpose:

Creating a vision board is a powerful way to engage in active self-affirmation. By regularly engaging with the visual representation of your worth, you reinforce the positive beliefs you are cultivating about yourself (Harter, 2012; Brown, 2012).

These exercises focus on enhancing self-love and self-worth, both critical aspects of moving toward secure attachment. Through affirmations and creative visualizations, you reinforce your belief in your own value and work toward emotional independence, which is essential for healthier, more secure relationships with others.

CHAPTER 7: HEALING ATTACHMENT WOUNDS: UNDERSTANDING AND OVERCOMING TRAUMA

"The wounds of attachment are often invisible, but they impact every aspect of our emotional lives. Healing them begins with understanding."

Introduction to Chapter 7: Healing Attachment Wounds
In this chapter, we explore the journey of healing from attachment trauma, particularly for those with an anxious attachment style. Attachment wounds, often rooted in early experiences of neglect, inconsistency, or emotional unavailability, can deeply impact our relationships and emotional well-being.

Understanding how attachment trauma affects us is an essential first step toward recovery.

Before we begin, it is important to note that I am not a medical or mental health professional. The information shared in this chapter is based on personal experience and research. While these insights can provide guidance and encouragement, it is essential to recognize that trauma and attachment issues can be complex, and some cases are best treated with the support of a licensed therapist or counselor. If you feel overwhelmed or experience significant distress while reading, I strongly encourage you to seek professional help. Trauma-informed therapies, such as Emotionally Focused Therapy (EFT), Trauma-Focused Cognitive Behavioral Therapy (TF-CBT), and other specialized treatments, are proven to help individuals heal from attachment wounds (Johnson, 2004; van der Kolk, 2014).

This chapter provides tools and exercises to help you understand the nature of attachment trauma and how it may affect your life. By exploring your past experiences, developing healthier emotional regulation strategies, and practicing self-compassion, you can begin to heal the wounds that have shaped your emotional patterns. However, healing from trauma is a process, and while self-help practices are valuable, they are not a substitute for professional guidance when needed.

Let's begin this journey of healing with understanding and compassion for ourselves and others.

Understanding Attachment Trauma

Attachment trauma refers to the emotional wounds that develop when a child experiences disruptions in their early attachment relationships, particularly with primary caregivers. These disruptions can stem from neglect, abuse, inconsistent caregiving, or emotional unavailability, which can create deep, lasting scars in the individual's ability to form secure attachments later in life. Attachment trauma is a central issue for those with anxious attachment because it often involves unresolved fears of rejection, abandonment, or inadequacy (Bowlby, 1969; van der Kolk, 2014).

Trauma experienced in early attachment relationships can create a pattern where individuals develop heightened sensitivity to emotional cues, interpret neutral or ambiguous situations as threats, and struggle to trust others. These behaviors, while initially adaptive as survival mechanisms, can become maladaptive in adult relationships, leading to anxiety, insecurity, and difficulty with emotional regulation (Mikulincer & Shaver, 2007). Understanding how attachment trauma manifests is the first step in healing these wounds.

The Impact of Childhood Attachment Trauma

Attachment trauma doesn't always manifest as dramatic or obvious incidents; it often presents as subtle patterns of emotional neglect or inconsistencies in caregiving. For example, a parent who is emotionally unavailable or inconsistent in meeting the child's needs may create an insecure attachment. These children may grow up feeling that their needs will not be met, which can manifest in adulthood as heightened anxiety or fear in relationships.

For individuals with anxious attachment, these early experiences may have created a foundation where they are constantly seeking reassurance, have difficulty trusting others, and often feel unworthy of love or affection. This "attachment insecurity" affects their self-esteem and the way they interact with others, often leading to behaviors like over-analyzing situations, fearing abandonment, and having difficulty setting boundaries (Hazan & Shaver, 1987).

One example of attachment trauma might be a child raised in an unpredictable environment where their caregiver's emotional state fluctuated from nurturing to neglectful. As an adult, this person might find themselves excessively seeking attention or approval from their partners, fearing rejection at every turn.

The Neuroscience of Attachment Trauma

Attachment trauma has a profound effect on the brain, particularly the areas associated with emotional regulation, stress response, and social connection. Studies show that individuals with a history of attachment trauma often exhibit increased activation in the amygdala (the brain's emotional center) in response to stress or perceived threats (Schore, 2003). Additionally, chronic stress and unresolved trauma can alter the functioning of the prefrontal cortex, the brain region responsible for reasoning and impulse control, making it more difficult to manage emotions in a balanced way (Perry, 2001).

Understanding this brain-body connection is vital for individuals with anxious attachment, as it helps explain why they may experience intense emotional reactions to seemingly small triggers. By understanding the neurological basis of their responses, individuals can begin to normalize their reactions and approach healing with greater compassion and patience for themselves (Siegel, 2007).

Healing from Attachment Trauma: Steps Toward Recovery

Healing attachment trauma is a process that involves both emotional and psychological work. It requires individuals to develop new patterns of thinking, behaving, and interacting in relationships. The following steps outline a pathway to healing:

1. Acknowledge and Validate the Trauma: The first step in healing is to acknowledge that attachment trauma exists and that it has had a significant impact on your emotional life. This may involve recognizing that certain fears, insecurities, or relationship patterns are not inherent to you, but are the result of past wounds. Validation is key to healing because it allows individuals to accept their experiences without judgment or shame (van der Kolk, 2014). For example, someone may realize that their constant

need for reassurance in relationships stems from a childhood experience of emotional neglect.

2. Cultivate Self-Compassion: Healing attachment wounds requires a shift from self-criticism to self-compassion. Instead of blaming yourself for anxious or insecure feelings, treat yourself with kindness and understanding. Practicing self-compassion helps soothe the nervous system and enables you to approach healing from a place of self-care rather than self-blame (Neff, 2011). An example would be someone practicing self-compassion by acknowledging that their fears of abandonment are rooted in past trauma and that they deserve love and patience as they heal.

3. Create Safety in Relationships: In order to heal attachment wounds, it is crucial to establish relationships that offer safety and consistency. This might mean seeking out a therapist or counselor who is trauma-informed and can help you process past experiences. It also involves communicating your needs clearly with trusted partners, setting boundaries, and asking for reassurance in healthy, non-overwhelming ways. Having a partner who understands your attachment needs and can respond with empathy and patience is essential to this process.

4. Practice Mindfulness and Emotional Regulation: Individuals with attachment trauma often struggle with emotional regulation, experiencing intense emotions that can feel overwhelming. Mindfulness practices, such as meditation and deep breathing, can help you create space between a triggering event and your emotional response, allowing you to respond more calmly and thoughtfully. For example, practicing mindful breathing before reacting to a perceived abandonment can help reduce anxiety and increase emotional resilience (Kabat-Zinn, 1990).

5. Address and Reframe Core Beliefs: Attachment trauma often involves deeply ingrained core beliefs, such as “I am not worthy of love” or “I cannot trust others.” These beliefs can be reframed through cognitive-behavioral therapy (CBT), which

helps individuals challenge negative thoughts and replace them with healthier, more realistic beliefs. For example, if someone believes that they are unworthy of love, they can challenge that belief by identifying their positive qualities and reflecting on times when they received love and support.

The Role of Therapy in Healing Attachment Trauma

Therapy can be an essential tool in healing attachment trauma. Specific therapeutic approaches, such as Emotionally Focused Therapy (EFT), Attachment-Based Therapy, and Trauma-Focused Cognitive Behavioral Therapy (TF-CBT), are designed to help individuals process attachment injuries and rebuild their ability to trust and connect with others. These therapies provide a safe, structured environment where individuals can explore their past experiences, challenge their emotional responses, and learn healthier ways of relating.

For example, in EFT, the therapist helps individuals and couples understand the underlying attachment needs driving their emotional responses, fostering more secure and connected relationships (Johnson, 2004). Therapy also offers individuals the opportunity to work through past trauma in a supportive setting, often facilitating profound healing and transformation.

Example Case: Healing Attachment Trauma

Sarah, a 35-year-old woman, had a history of anxious attachment in her relationships. She found herself constantly seeking reassurance from her partners and feeling intensely afraid of abandonment. Through therapy, Sarah uncovered that her attachment anxieties were rooted in early childhood experiences of emotional neglect. Her mother was emotionally distant, and Sarah often felt alone and unsupported.

Over time, Sarah learned how to regulate her emotions through mindfulness practices and began challenging her negative beliefs about herself. With her therapist's guidance, she reframed her belief that she was unworthy of love and began to practice self-compassion. As she built her sense of self-worth and started to create healthier relationships, her fears of abandonment lessened, and she began to experience more stable, fulfilling connections.

Conclusion: Moving Beyond Trauma

Healing attachment trauma is not an easy process, but it is a deeply transformative one. By acknowledging the impact of early attachment wounds, cultivating self-compassion, and rebuilding trust in relationships, individuals with anxious attachment can begin to heal the past and move toward secure attachment. The journey requires patience, support, and commitment, but the rewards—a greater sense of self-worth, healthier relationships, and emotional resilience—are well worth the effort.

CHAPTER 7 FOLLOW UP EXERCISES:

Exercise 1: "The Timeline Of Healing"

This exercise helps you visualize and map out your healing journey, providing a clearer understanding of how attachment trauma has influenced your past and can empower your future. By creating a timeline, you gain insight into your emotional evolution and can track your progress toward healing.

Please note: I am not a medical professional. This exercise is based on personal experience and research, and is intended as a self-help tool. If you are experiencing significant emotional distress, please seek guidance from a licensed mental health professional.

Steps:

1. Create Your Timeline: Take a blank sheet of paper or a digital document and draw a horizontal line across the page, with the left side representing your past and the right side your present and future.

2. Identify Key Events: Mark significant events related to your attachment experiences along the timeline. These could include moments when you felt particularly neglected, rejected, or unsupported, as well as instances of healing or breakthrough. Label these events with brief descriptions (e.g., "Childhood neglect," "First significant relationship," "Therapy breakthrough").

3. Reflect on Patterns: After marking these key events, take a moment to reflect on any patterns you see in how attachment

trauma has shaped your relationships. Are there recurring themes of abandonment, fear, or emotional neglect? Are there positive turning points, such as support from trusted individuals or significant self-discovery moments?

4. Visualize Healing: On the right side of the timeline, write or draw what healing looks like for you moving forward. What changes in your behavior and emotions do you hope to see? How will your future relationships look once you've worked through your attachment trauma? Create a clear vision of hope and progress.

5. Review Regularly: Revisit this timeline every few months to assess your progress. Celebrate the milestones you have reached, no matter how small, and use the visual representation of your journey to stay motivated and inspired in your healing process.

Purpose:

This exercise helps you acknowledge the full scope of your healing journey. By visualizing the path from trauma to healing, you reinforce the idea that recovery is possible and progress is tangible (Mikulincer & Shaver, 2007).

Exercise 2: "The Trust Rebuilding Journal"

Rebuilding trust—both in yourself and in others—is a vital part of healing attachment trauma. This exercise encourages you to reflect on and document instances in which you can build or strengthen trust, starting with small, manageable steps.

Please note: This exercise is based on my personal experiences and research into attachment healing. It is not intended as a substitute for professional medical or psychological advice. If you find you are struggling significantly, it is important to seek support from a licensed professional.

Steps:

1. Create Your Trust Journal: Use a journal or digital tool to start tracking moments throughout your day or week when you build or strengthen trust. These might be moments where you challenge old patterns or allow yourself to trust others in small ways.

2. Identify Trust-Building Moments: Each time you engage in an act of trust—whether it's trusting a friend with a vulnerable moment, setting a boundary in a relationship, or choosing to trust your own feelings—record the event in your journal. Include details such as:

* What happened?

* How did you feel before, during, and after the event?

* What was the outcome? Did you feel more secure afterward?

3. Reflect on Your Fears: Alongside these positive entries, also acknowledge any fears or discomforts you may have had around trust. For example, if you were hesitant to trust someone but chose to anyway, write about the fears you overcame and the lessons learned.

4. Evaluate Growth: After a few weeks of journaling, review your entries. Do you notice a shift in your ability to trust? Are there patterns of small successes that have led to greater confidence in your relationships? Reflect on how trust is gradually being rebuilt in your life, both internally and with others.

5. Set Intentions for Growth: Based on your reflections, set new goals for building trust. For example, if you've found that being vulnerable with a close friend has helped, you might set the intention to continue that practice. Or, if you've struggled with trusting a partner, you might focus on reinforcing trust with small actions of consistency or reassurance.

Purpose:

The Trust Rebuilding Journal is designed to help you focus on progress rather than perfection. By tracking your trust-building moments and reflecting on both successes and challenges, you encourage yourself to take manageable steps toward restoring faith in your relationships (Hazan & Shaver, 1987; Siegel, 2007).

CHAPTER 8: MOVING FORWARD—BUILDING SECURE ATTACHMENTS IN ADULT RELATIONSHIPS

"You yourself, as much as anybody in the entire universe, deserve your love and affection."
— Buddha

In this chapter, we explore how individuals with anxious attachment can cultivate secure attachments in their adult relationships. Building a secure attachment style, especially when you've experienced trauma or emotional neglect in childhood, is not only possible but crucial for developing healthy, fulfilling connections with others. Secure attachment promotes emotional stability, healthier communication, and greater trust, all of which are essential for nurturing lasting and meaningful relationships.

Before diving into the tools and exercises for building secure attachments, it's important to note that healing attachment trauma is a gradual process that requires patience, self-compassion, and a willingness to engage in healthy relationship patterns. It also requires unlearning old habits that may have been protective but are no longer serving you in adulthood. Building a secure attachment style is not an immediate fix, but over time, consistent effort can lead to profound transformation in how you relate to others.

Understanding Secure Attachment in Adulthood

To create secure attachments in adult relationships, it's important to first understand what a secure attachment style looks like. Securely attached individuals tend to have a positive view of themselves and others. They are comfortable with intimacy, can express their needs clearly, and can rely on others without fear of rejection. Secure attachment fosters healthy boundaries and communication, while also allowing for interdependence rather than unhealthy dependence or emotional avoidance (Hazan & Shaver, 1987).

For someone with anxious attachment, adopting these behaviors can feel daunting, especially if they've experienced rejection or abandonment in the past. The key is not to demand perfection from yourself, but to set small, achievable goals for improving emotional regulation, communication, and trust. With consistency, these changes can strengthen your capacity to form more secure, stable connections.

The Role of Vulnerability and Trust

Vulnerability and trust are foundational elements of secure attachment. It is often difficult for those with anxious attachment to open up fully because of the fear of being hurt or abandoned again. Yet, it is through vulnerability that authentic connections are formed. Trust is built over time by demonstrating consistency, empathy, and openness in relationships (Johnson, 2004).

A key component in overcoming the anxiety surrounding vulnerability is learning how to tolerate the discomfort of being emotionally open without pushing others away or becoming overly clingy. This balance of trust and vulnerability can be challenging but is essential for creating intimacy and security within relationships. According to Siegel (2007), fostering secure attachment requires creating a safe space where both partners feel seen, heard, and supported.

Addressing the Impact of Past Attachment Wounds

Healing from attachment trauma involves acknowledging the emotional wounds of the past and learning how those experiences shape current behaviors. Often, individuals with anxious attachment bring unresolved fears and patterns from childhood into their adult relationships. These fears can lead to behaviors such as excessive reassurance-seeking, difficulty with boundaries, or emotional volatility in the face of perceived threats (Shaver & Mikulincer, 2002).

Understanding the root causes of these behaviors is a powerful step toward healing. Therapy, particularly therapies designed to address attachment and trauma, can be immensely helpful in exploring these early wounds and creating space for emotional growth. For those not in therapy, journaling, self-reflection, and mindfulness practices can also provide insight into how past wounds affect current behaviors and can help mitigate their impact (van der Kolk, 2014).

Building Secure Attachment: Practical Steps

1. Cultivating Emotional Regulation: A key feature of secure attachment is the ability to regulate emotions effectively, especially in challenging or stressful situations. Individuals with anxious attachment often struggle with emotional dysregulation, which can lead to impulsive behaviors or exaggerated emotional

reactions (Mikulincer & Shaver, 2007). To build emotional regulation, practice mindfulness, deep breathing exercises, and grounding techniques to stay calm during emotional triggers.

2. Communicating Needs Clearly: Anxiously attached individuals often struggle to communicate their needs in healthy ways. Learning how to assertively express your feelings and needs without resorting to desperation or silence is crucial for fostering secure connections. Practice using "I" statements to express how you feel and what you need, avoiding blame or criticism of the other person (Johnson, 2004).

3. Building Trust Gradually: Trust-building in relationships is a gradual process that requires consistency and transparency. For those with anxious attachment, this may involve working through fears of abandonment by focusing on the present moment rather than worrying about future rejection. In relationships, show up consistently and supportively, and allow yourself to see that trust can be built slowly over time.

4. Setting Healthy Boundaries: Secure attachment thrives in relationships where both individuals respect each other's emotional boundaries. For someone with anxious attachment, learning to set and maintain healthy boundaries may be a challenge, as it requires balancing the desire for closeness with the need for autonomy. Establish clear, respectful boundaries with others and honor your own needs for space and self-care.

5. Seeking Support When Needed: Healing attachment wounds and building secure attachment styles may require professional guidance. If you find yourself struggling with intense emotional reactions or patterns that seem difficult to break, consider seeking therapy with a professional trained in attachment theory. Cognitive Behavioral Therapy (CBT) or Emotionally Focused Therapy (EFT) can be particularly beneficial for individuals with attachment-related concerns (Johnson, 2004).

Conclusion

Building secure attachments in adult relationships is a

powerful, transformative process that requires time, effort, and a willingness to confront old wounds. While the path may be challenging at times, the rewards of secure attachment—deeper intimacy, emotional stability, and healthier relationships—are well worth the effort. Remember, healing is a journey, and you do not have to do it alone. Whether through therapy, self-reflection, or support from loved ones, you can take steps every day to build more secure, fulfilling connections.

Example: Secure Attachment Daily Reflection

Let's say I recently noticed that in my relationships, particularly with close friends, I often feel the need for constant reassurance that I'm valued or loved. In one instance, I texted a friend multiple times asking if they were upset with me because I hadn't heard back from them in a few hours, even though they usually take their time to respond.

After reviewing this situation through the Secure Attachment Daily Reflection exercise, I realized that my need for reassurance came from a deep-rooted fear of abandonment, stemming from childhood experiences where I felt emotionally neglected. Reflecting on my emotional state, I acknowledged that my anxiety was triggered by not hearing from my friend in a timely manner, despite knowing they had a busy schedule.

For the next day, I set a goal to practice calming techniques—such as deep breathing and mindfulness—before I texted anyone. I reminded myself that my worth is not dependent on receiving immediate responses. By acknowledging this and making the conscious choice not to send a message, I gradually built more emotional stability and started trusting the other person's space and autonomy.

CHAPTER 8 FOLLOW UP EXERCISES:

Exercise 1: "The Secure Attachment Daily Reflection"

This exercise encourages you to reflect daily on your emotional responses and behaviors within your relationships. By tracking how you engage with others, you'll be able to identify patterns and make small adjustments to build a more secure attachment style. Over time, this will help you develop greater emotional awareness and healthier communication.

Steps:

1. Set Aside Time for Reflection: Dedicate 10–15 minutes each day for this reflection. You can do this at the end of the day or after a significant interaction with someone close to you.

2. Assess Your Emotional Responses: Reflect on your emotional responses throughout the day. How did you feel during interactions with others? Were you able to maintain a calm and balanced state, or did you experience anxiety, frustration, or fear? Write down specific situations where you noticed these emotional shifts.

3. Evaluate Your Attachment-Related Behaviors: After identifying emotional responses, consider how you responded behaviorally in these moments. Did you reach out for reassurance, shut down emotionally, or express your feelings in a healthy way? Write down any patterns you notice in how you engage with others

based on attachment-related triggers.

4. Track Positive Changes: Each day, identify at least one moment where you handled an attachment-related issue more securely—whether it was by expressing yourself more calmly, respecting your boundaries, or managing anxiety. Write this down as a reminder of the positive steps you've taken toward building a more secure attachment.

5. Set Goals for the Next Day: Based on your reflections, set one intention for the following day. This might involve making an effort to communicate more openly, practice active listening, or set a boundary with someone. Each goal should be realistic and achievable.

Purpose:

The goal of this exercise is to enhance your self-awareness and provide daily opportunities to practice building secure attachment behaviors. By tracking your progress and identifying areas for improvement, you can gradually strengthen your emotional regulation and relational skills (Shaver & Mikulincer, 2002; Siegel, 2007).

Exercise 2: "The Attachment Role-Playing Practice"

Role-playing allows you to experiment with secure attachment behaviors in a safe, controlled environment. This exercise involves practicing healthy communication and boundary-setting skills by taking on different roles in your relationships, helping you rehearse positive behaviors before applying them in real-life situations.

Steps:

1. Identify a Relationship Challenge: Think of a situation in one of your relationships where you struggle with attachment-related behaviors. This could be difficulty setting boundaries, expressing your needs, or managing anxiety about rejection. Write down the specific challenge you're facing.

2. Choose Your Roles: For this exercise, you'll need a partner (a friend, therapist, or trusted individual) who is willing to engage in role-play with you. You'll take turns playing different roles. One person will act as you, and the other will play the role of the person with whom you are having difficulty. For example, if you're anxious about setting boundaries with a partner, one person can play you while the other plays your partner.

3. Act Out the Scenario: Role-play the interaction using secure attachment behaviors. For example, if you struggle with expressing needs, practice calmly stating your feelings and asking for support without apologizing or minimizing your needs. If you're working on trust-building, practice responding to emotional vulnerability with empathy and validation.

4. Switch Roles: After the first round of role-play, switch roles so that each person has the chance to practice both perspectives. Pay attention to how each role feels and identify moments where you felt more or less secure in the interaction.

5. Debrief and Reflect: After completing the role-play, take time to discuss how it went. Reflect on what felt challenging and what felt

empowering. Did you feel more comfortable expressing yourself or setting boundaries? What behaviors could you adopt in real-life situations to make your attachment style more secure?

Purpose:

Role-playing helps you practice key skills such as assertiveness, communication, and emotional regulation in a low-pressure environment. It also allows you to reframe your approach to relational challenges, fostering a sense of empowerment and confidence in handling difficult situations (Johnson, 2004; Mikulincer & Shaver, 2007).

CHAPTER 9: CULTIVATING EMOTIONAL RESILIENCE—BOUNCING BACK FROM SETBACKS

"The greatest glory in living lies not in never falling, but in rising every time we fall."
— Nelson Mandela

Emotional resilience is the ability to bounce back from adversity, challenges, and stressors in a healthy way. For individuals with an anxious attachment style, cultivating emotional resilience is particularly crucial. When faced with relationship challenges, rejection, or feelings of inadequacy, it's easy to slip into old patterns of overthinking, emotional dysregulation, or withdrawal. However, resilience empowers us to cope more effectively, bounce back from setbacks, and continue moving forward with a stronger sense of self.

In this chapter, we will explore the key components of emotional resilience, how attachment trauma impacts resilience, and practical strategies for building resilience in the face of difficult emotions and relationship challenges. Resilience isn't about avoiding pain but about learning to navigate it with strength and self-compassion, and it is a skill that can be cultivated over time.

Understanding Emotional Resilience

Emotional resilience involves several core elements, including emotional regulation, adaptability, optimism, and a sense of self-efficacy (Bonanno, 2004). It allows individuals to face life's challenges and recover from them without losing hope or falling into unhealthy patterns. Resilience doesn't mean you won't feel hurt, sadness, or anger, but rather that you have the capacity to process these emotions and eventually move forward.

For individuals with anxious attachment, emotional resilience can be more challenging to cultivate. The tendency toward anxiety and emotional dependence can make setbacks feel like insurmountable obstacles. However, just as attachment styles are learned and can be changed, so too can emotional resilience be developed. By understanding the root causes of your emotional reactions and practicing resilience-building strategies, you can start to shift your emotional responses and build a greater sense of emotional stability.

The Impact of Attachment Trauma on Resilience

Attachment trauma, especially in childhood, can significantly impact emotional resilience in adulthood. Those who experienced inconsistent caregiving or emotional neglect may have developed an attachment style that is hyper-vigilant or reactive to perceived emotional threats (Siegel, 2007). As a result, when faced with emotional distress or relationship challenges, individuals with anxious attachment may feel overwhelmed by their emotions and struggle to recover.

Research on attachment theory suggests that early experiences of being supported, understood, and cared for foster the development of secure attachment, which in turn supports emotional resilience (Mikulincer & Shaver, 2007). Conversely, those with insecure attachment styles—particularly anxious attachment—may struggle to self-soothe or regulate their emotions effectively when faced with emotional challenges (Hazan & Shaver, 1987).

However, this doesn't mean that emotional resilience cannot be cultivated. By developing self-awareness, practicing mindfulness, and learning healthy emotional regulation techniques, individuals with anxious attachment can significantly improve their ability to cope with difficult emotions and setbacks.

Strategies for Building Emotional Resilience

1. Develop Self-Compassion: One of the first steps in cultivating resilience is developing self-compassion. For someone with anxious attachment, self-criticism and fear of rejection can be paralyzing. Learning to treat yourself with kindness and understanding during moments of difficulty is essential. Kristin Neff (2011) defines self-compassion as the ability to offer oneself the same kindness and care that one would offer a close friend. Practicing self-compassion helps reduce emotional distress and enhances resilience by fostering a positive relationship with oneself.

2. Practice Emotional Regulation Techniques: Emotional regulation is the ability to manage your emotional responses to stressors, and it's a cornerstone of emotional resilience. Techniques such as deep breathing, progressive muscle relaxation, and mindfulness can help individuals manage their emotions and reduce the intensity of anxiety or sadness. Research has shown that mindfulness meditation, in particular, can enhance emotional regulation by promoting awareness of emotional states and allowing for a non-judgmental response

(Siegel, 2007).

3. Challenge Negative Thought Patterns: Anxiously attached individuals often experience negative, automatic thoughts that fuel feelings of insecurity or inadequacy. These thoughts can prevent emotional recovery by reinforcing feelings of hopelessness or unworthiness. Cognitive Behavioral Therapy (CBT) is an effective tool for challenging and reframing these negative thoughts (Beck, 2011). By identifying cognitive distortions—such as catastrophizing or black-and-white thinking —you can begin to break the cycle of self-defeating beliefs and replace them with more balanced, realistic perspectives.

4. Establish Strong Support Networks: Resilience is not about handling everything on your own; it's about knowing when and how to seek support. Building strong, supportive relationships with friends, family, or a therapist can significantly improve your emotional resilience. Having someone to talk to during difficult times can provide validation, perspective, and emotional support, all of which are critical for emotional recovery (Hazan & Shaver, 1987).

5. Reframe Setbacks as Opportunities for Growth: In the face of challenges or setbacks, it can be easy to fall into a mindset of defeat. However, resilience is about seeing setbacks not as failures but as opportunities for growth. By reframing your struggles as learning experiences, you can develop a more optimistic outlook and build the strength to move forward. For example, instead of viewing a conflict with a partner as a sign that the relationship is doomed, you could view it as an opportunity to practice communication and emotional regulation.

Personal Example: Building Resilience After a Relationship Setback

A few years ago, I faced a particularly challenging situation in my relationship with a close friend. We had a misunderstanding that led to a period of emotional distance between us. As someone with anxious attachment, my first instinct was to spiral into thoughts of rejection and fear that the relationship was over. I felt overwhelmed by feelings of sadness, frustration, and helplessness.

However, I decided to use the strategies for building resilience outlined above. First, I practiced self-compassion by acknowledging that it was okay to feel upset and that my feelings didn't mean I had lost the friendship. I allowed myself to sit with the discomfort without rushing to fix things. I also reached out to another close friend to talk about my feelings, which helped me gain perspective and emotional support. Through mindfulness and deep breathing, I was able to calm my anxiety and give myself the space to think clearly.

Eventually, I communicated openly with my friend, expressing my feelings without blaming or accusing. We worked through the misunderstanding together and grew stronger as a result. This experience was a powerful reminder that setbacks don't define me, and that resilience is about finding strength in vulnerability and openness.

Conclusion

Emotional resilience is a key factor in overcoming setbacks and building healthier, more secure relationships. For individuals with anxious attachment, resilience-building requires a combination of self-compassion, emotional regulation, and supportive relationships. By practicing these strategies consistently, you can increase your ability to cope with challenges, bounce back from setbacks, and ultimately create a more stable, positive attachment style in your relationships.

CHAPTER 9 FOLLOW UP EXPERCISES:

Exercise 1: "Resilience In Action—The 5-Minute Emotional Reset"

This exercise helps you develop the ability to quickly manage emotional distress in the moment. By practicing this "reset" technique, you can build emotional resilience by learning to reframe challenging situations and regulate your emotional responses in real-time.

Steps:

1. Identify the Emotional Trigger: The next time you experience an emotional trigger—such as frustration in a conversation, feeling rejected, or anxiety about a situation—take a moment to notice the emotion that's arising.

2. Pause and Breathe: Take a deep breath, hold it for three seconds, then slowly exhale. Repeat this three times. As you breathe, try to detach from the emotional reaction and observe it without judgment. You are not trying to eliminate the emotion, but rather, create space between the trigger and your response.

3. Reframe the Situation: Ask yourself: Is there a more balanced way to interpret this situation? For example, if you feel ignored by a friend's delayed response, reframe the thought from "They don't care about me" to "They may be busy, and it doesn't reflect their feelings toward me." Remind yourself that not all challenges need to be perceived as threats.

4. Engage in a Grounding Activity: If you feel yourself still struggling with the emotion, engage in a brief grounding activity. This could be gently squeezing a stress ball, noticing the details of an object in your environment, or briefly stepping outside for a change of scenery.

5. Check In with Your Feelings: After completing the exercise, ask yourself: Do I feel calmer? What has shifted in my emotional state? Take a moment to reflect and notice any changes in your emotional response.

Purpose:

This exercise strengthens your emotional resilience by helping you reset quickly and gain control over emotional reactions. It encourages self-regulation and mindfulness, both of which are crucial for bouncing back from emotional distress (Siegel, 2007; Neff, 2011).

CHAPTER 9 FOLLOW UP EXERCISES:

Exercise 2: "Resilience Revisited—Tracking Emotional Growth"

This longer-term exercise focuses on tracking your emotional growth and resilience over time. By identifying patterns in how you handle setbacks and emotionally challenging situations, you can see how much progress you've made and where additional focus is needed.

Steps:

1. Create a Resilience Journal: Start a journal dedicated to tracking your emotional responses and resilience-building efforts. Each entry should include a brief description of a challenging situation you encountered, your emotional response, and the strategies you used to cope.

2. Record Emotional Patterns: Over time, look for recurring themes in your responses. Are there situations that consistently trigger anxiety or defensiveness? Are you able to reset and bounce back more quickly as time passes? Note these patterns.

3. Evaluate Your Coping Strategies: Reflect on which emotional resilience strategies have been the most effective for you (e.g., deep breathing, self-compassion, seeking support from others). Consider any strategies that you haven't yet tried or feel you could integrate more consistently into your routine.

4. Set Monthly Goals for Growth: At the end of each month, set one resilience goal for yourself based on your observations. This could be something like practicing mindfulness daily, setting clearer boundaries, or learning to reframe negative thoughts more effectively.

5. Celebrate Your Progress: Each time you make a breakthrough or manage a difficult emotion more effectively than before, acknowledge and celebrate your progress. This could be as simple as writing down a positive affirmation or reflecting on the growth you've experienced.

Purpose:

This exercise helps you track and assess your emotional resilience development over time. By setting goals, tracking patterns, and celebrating progress, you reinforce the skills and behaviors that foster resilience, building confidence in your ability to handle future challenges (Bonanno, 2004; Beck, 2011).

Both exercises aim to cultivate emotional resilience in different ways: one focuses on real-time emotional regulation, while the other encourages a reflective, long-term approach to tracking and building emotional strength. Together, they create a dynamic toolkit for managing setbacks and fostering emotional growth.

CHAPTER 10: BUILDING LONG-TERM EMOTIONAL RESILIENCE

"A secure attachment is the bedrock of all healthy relationships."
— Dr. John Bowlby, founder of Attachment Theory

Building emotional resilience is essential for maintaining well-being and navigating life's challenges. Resilience is not about avoiding adversity but developing the capacity to face and grow through difficult experiences. For those with anxious attachment, cultivating resilience is particularly important because it helps break the cycle of emotional dependence and reactivity that often characterizes anxious relationships.

In this chapter, we will discuss how you can build emotional resilience over the long term, using strategies and tools that empower you to navigate relationship challenges and personal setbacks with strength. This journey toward resilience is about shifting from a reactive, fear-driven mindset to a proactive, growth-oriented one, grounded in emotional awareness and self-regulation.

The Science of Emotional Resilience

Emotional resilience is the ability to adapt and recover from life's difficulties. This includes managing emotions, developing coping strategies, and maintaining a sense of optimism and hope, even in the face of adversity (Bonanno, 2004). For individuals with an anxious attachment style, emotional resilience may be harder to cultivate because they may tend to overreact to emotional stressors or become overwhelmed by the fear of abandonment.

Research shows that individuals with secure attachment styles tend to display higher emotional resilience because they have a strong internal sense of safety and self-worth (Mikulincer & Shaver, 2007). In contrast, those with insecure attachment styles, including anxious attachment, may struggle with emotional regulation, making it harder to manage feelings of anxiety, fear, or sadness when faced with relationship or life stressors (Hazan & Shaver, 1987).

However, emotional resilience is a skill that can be learned. Through consistent practice, anyone can enhance their emotional capacity to handle stress, setbacks, and difficulties with greater self-control and emotional insight.

The Importance of Self-Regulation in Emotional Resilience

Self-regulation—the ability to control one's emotions, thoughts, and behaviors in the face of challenges—is a cornerstone of emotional resilience. Self-regulation allows you to pause and choose a thoughtful, measured response, rather than reacting impulsively or out of fear. For individuals with anxious attachment, this may involve learning to manage anxiety and shift from a place of emotional reactivity to one of emotional awareness and control.

For example, let's say you find yourself feeling overwhelmed after a conversation with your partner, during which they said something that triggered feelings of insecurity or fear of abandonment. Your natural instinct might be to immediately seek reassurance or become upset. However, through emotional regulation techniques such as deep breathing, mindfulness, or positive self-talk, you can create a space between the trigger and your response. By practicing emotional regulation, you can approach the situation more calmly, allowing for healthier communication and a more resilient reaction.

Practical Strategies for Building Emotional Resilience

Practice Mindfulness: Mindfulness is the practice of staying present in the moment without judgment. Research shows that mindfulness improves emotional regulation, enhances self-awareness, and fosters resilience (Siegel, 2007). By practicing mindfulness regularly, you can become more aware of your emotional triggers and learn to respond thoughtfully, rather than react impulsively. You can start with short, five-minute mindfulness exercises—such as focusing on your breath or engaging in mindful walking—and gradually increase the time as you become more comfortable.

Reframe Negative Thoughts: One of the biggest challenges for those with anxious attachment is a tendency to engage in negative thought patterns, especially when faced with emotional stress. Cognitive Behavioral Therapy (CBT) research shows that reframing negative thoughts is an effective strategy for increasing resilience (Beck, 2011). For example, if you think "I'm not good enough for my partner," you can reframe this thought to "I have valuable qualities that my partner appreciates." By challenging these automatic negative thoughts, you can shift your perspective and reduce emotional distress.

Develop a Support Network: Having a strong support system is critical for building emotional resilience. Research indicates that emotional support from others buffers the impact of stress and fosters resilience (Mikulincer & Shaver, 2007). Surrounding yourself with supportive friends, family, or a therapist can provide validation, comfort, and perspective when you are struggling. A secure support system is a lifeline when you need reassurance, encouragement, or just a safe space to express your feelings.

Cultivate Self-Compassion: Self-compassion involves treating yourself with the same kindness and understanding that you would offer to a close friend. For people with anxious attachment, this means recognizing your emotional pain without judgment and offering yourself empathy rather than self-criticism. Kristin Neff (2011) highlights that self-compassion is essential for resilience, as it allows you to acknowledge difficult emotions without getting overwhelmed by them.

Engage in Resilience-Building Activities: Finally, engaging in activities that promote overall well-being—such as exercise, creative pursuits, or spending time in nature—can enhance emotional resilience. These activities promote the release of endorphins and reduce the physiological effects of stress, making it easier to manage emotional turbulence.

Personal Example: Building Resilience After a Relationship Conflict

I had a personal experience where my partner and I had

a disagreement that triggered feelings of abandonment and anxiety within me. In the past, I would have spiraled into fear, seeking constant reassurance, or even withdrawing emotionally to protect myself from further hurt. However, this time, I decided to approach the situation differently.

I first practiced mindfulness by focusing on my breath for a few minutes to calm my nervous system. Instead of immediately reacting, I gave myself the space to process my emotions. I realized that the disagreement was not about the value of our relationship but rather a miscommunication that triggered old fears within me. I then reframed my initial thoughts—shifting from "I'm unworthy of love" to "This is just a temporary challenge, and it doesn't reflect my worth." After taking some time to self-soothe, I reached out to my partner, communicated my feelings calmly, and listened to their perspective. The situation ultimately deepened our understanding of each other, and we were able to resolve the conflict more constructively.

Through this experience, I learned that emotional resilience is built through practice. By using mindfulness, reframing my thoughts, and self-regulating my emotions, I was able to recover from the conflict without letting it erode my sense of self-worth or my relationship.

Conclusion

Building emotional resilience is an ongoing process that requires practice, patience, and commitment. For individuals with anxious attachment, developing resilience involves learning to manage anxiety, regulate emotions, and respond to challenges in healthier ways. By incorporating mindfulness, reframing negative thoughts, seeking support, and cultivating self-compassion, you can gradually strengthen your emotional resilience and become better equipped to handle life's ups and downs.

CHAPTER 10 FOLLOW UP EXPERCISES:

Exercise 1: "Mindfulness Journal—Tracking Emotional Growth"

This exercise encourages self-awareness by tracking your emotional responses and resilience over time. Regular mindfulness journaling can help you see patterns in your emotional reactions and identify growth areas, allowing you to celebrate your progress and continue developing emotional resilience.

Steps:

1. Set Aside Time for Reflection: At the end of each day, spend 5-10 minutes reflecting on your emotional experiences. Write down any instances where you faced challenges or moments of emotional stress.

2. Identify Emotional Triggers: In your journal, note the specific situations or events that triggered emotional reactions (e.g., a difficult conversation, feeling misunderstood, a work deadline). Reflect on how you responded emotionally and whether that response was in alignment with your values and resilience goals.

3. Use Mindfulness Techniques: For each entry, note any mindfulness techniques you used (deep breathing, grounding exercises, or reframing thoughts). Evaluate whether these techniques helped regulate your emotions and promote resilience.

4. Assess Your Growth: Look at patterns over time. How have your emotional responses changed? Are you noticing quicker emotional recovery? Have your coping strategies evolved? Reflect on any areas where you still struggle and commit to practicing specific resilience techniques the next time similar emotions arise.

Purpose:

This exercise builds emotional awareness and strengthens your ability to track your growth, which is crucial for long-term emotional resilience. The practice of mindful reflection encourages you to take responsibility for your emotional state and actively engage in the process of self-regulation (Siegel, 2007; Neff, 2011).

Exercise 2: "Building Your Resilience Toolkit—Adding New Strategies"

In this exercise, you will expand your emotional resilience toolkit by experimenting with new strategies. By diversifying the techniques you use to manage stress and regulate emotions, you can build a more robust set of tools for navigating future challenges.

Steps:

1. Explore New Resilience Techniques: Research and select two new emotional resilience strategies to try. These could include practices such as progressive muscle relaxation, visualization exercises, or engaging in creative activities like journaling or painting.

2. Practice One Technique Daily: Commit to practicing one of the new techniques each day for a week. Make sure to dedicate at least 10 minutes to fully immerse yourself in the exercise. This could be during a time of stress, after a difficult conversation, or simply as a preventive measure.

3. Evaluate Your Experience: At the end of the week, assess how each technique impacted your emotional state. Did one of the techniques help you feel calmer? Did you notice any changes in your ability to respond more resiliently to stress?

4. Add the Most Effective Techniques to Your Toolkit: Choose the strategies that had the most positive impact and add them to your emotional resilience toolkit. Practice these regularly, alongside the other tools you've developed, to ensure that you always have multiple strategies at your disposal when needed.

Purpose:

This exercise encourages ongoing learning and experimentation with different resilience strategies. Building a diverse emotional toolkit ensures that you have a wide range of tools to draw on, helping you remain adaptable in the face of new challenges (Bonanno, 2004; Beck, 2011).

Both of these exercises aim to foster the development of emotional resilience in different ways: one focuses on mindful reflection and emotional tracking, while the other encourages you to diversify and expand your resilience-building techniques. Together, they support long-term growth in emotional resilience.

CHAPTER 11: EMBRACING YOUR JOURNEY OF EMOTIONAL RESILIENCE

"The journey to healing is not about perfection but about progress. By learning to understand and heal our attachment wounds, we can transform fear into security and vulnerability into strength."
— Author's Reflection

As we come to the end of this journey, I want to express my deepest gratitude for your commitment to building emotional resilience. This book has been a roadmap to help you face the difficulties that arise in relationships and in life with greater strength, wisdom, and self-awareness. Whether you've been working through an anxious attachment style or simply looking to cultivate deeper emotional resilience, I hope this journey has empowered you to navigate your emotional world with more grace, understanding, and self-compassion. Building emotional resilience isn't about achieving perfection or eliminating every emotional challenge. Rather, it's about acknowledging that pain and difficulty are part of the human experience and learning how to navigate them with a sense of calm, control, and connection. It's a lifelong practice, not a destination. Each step, whether big or small, contributes to your growth. As you've learned throughout this book, the key to emotional resilience lies in the ability to pause, reflect, and respond to difficult emotions in a way that honors your needs without losing sight of your worth.

I know firsthand how challenging it can be to break free from the patterns of fear and insecurity that come with anxious attachment. I, too, have experienced the overwhelming grip of anxiety, the fear of abandonment, and the desperate longing for reassurance. But I have also discovered that healing and resilience are possible, even when it feels like the road ahead is long and uncertain. In my own journey, the tools and strategies in this book have been transformative—mindfulness, emotional regulation, reframing negative thoughts, and self-compassion have all played pivotal roles in helping me build a more grounded, resilient sense of self.

It's important to remember that you are not alone in this process. Healing and growth are not linear, and there will be days when you feel uncertain or frustrated. But through every setback, you can rise, learn, and grow stronger. Surround yourself with people who support your growth and be kind to yourself in moments of struggle. Emotional resilience doesn't mean never feeling pain—it means learning to honor your emotions while keeping sight of your capacity for growth.

To those of you who have come to this book during a personal struggle, know that you are brave for taking the first step toward change. Healing is not a destination—it is a journey that requires patience, self-compassion, and commitment. Each time you face a challenge and choose to respond with emotional awareness and strength, you build the resilience that will carry you forward into a future where you are more empowered, more self-aware, and more able to navigate life's complexities with courage.

As you continue this journey, I encourage you to keep exploring the tools and exercises from this book. Implement them as best as you can, recognizing that no effort is too small. The more you practice self-compassion, emotional regulation, and mindfulness, the more resilient you will become. Over time, you will witness the transformation not just in how you react to challenges, but also in how you experience love, connection, and joy.

Remember, resilience isn't about being unshakable—it's about being able to bend without breaking. And you, with all your humanity, are more than capable of this. Keep going, because you have everything within you to build the emotional strength you need to thrive.

With heartfelt gratitude and support,

C.S.. VAIL

REFERENCES

Beck, A. T. (2011). Cognitive therapy: Basics and beyond (2nd ed.). Guilford Press.

Bonanno, G. A. (2004). Loss, trauma, and human resilience: Have we underestimated the human capacity to thrive after extremely aversive events? American Psychologist, 59(1), 20–28. https://doi.org/10.1037/0003-066X.59.1.20

Hazan, C., & Shaver, P. R. (1987). Romantic love conceptualized as an attachment process. Journal of Personality and Social Psychology, 52(3), 511–524. https://doi.org/10.1037/0022-3514.52.3.511

Mikulincer, M., & Shaver, P. R. (2007). Attachment in adulthood: Structure, dynamics, and change. Guilford Press.

Neff, K. D. (2011). Self-compassion: The proven power of being kind to yourself. William Morrow.

Siegel, D. J. (2007). The mindful brain: Reflection and attunement in the cultivation of well-being. W. W. Norton & Company.

www.ingramcontent.com/pod-product-compliance
Lightning Source LLC
LaVergne TN
LVHW010115170826
845678LV00012B/2419

* 9 7 9 8 2 1 8 5 6 9 5 6 3 *